# This book is presented to:

_____

# It was given to you by:

_____

# On this special day:

_____

YOU PRAY FOR ME, I'LL PRAY FOR YOU!

# YOU PRAY FOR ME, I'LL PRAY FOR YOU!

Tummy tickling stories and prayers we can read together

## Written and illustrated by
## Phil A. Smouse

**Standard**
PUBLISHING
*Bringing The Word to Life*™

Cincinnati, OH

# For Davey

Text and illustrations © 2006 Phil A. Smouse. © 2006 Standard Publishing, Cincinnati, Ohio. A division of Standex International Corporation. All rights reserved. Printed in China. Project editor: Lindsay Black. Cover design: Robert Glover. Scripture taken from the HOLY BIBLE, NEW INTERNATIONAL VERSION®. NIV®. Copyright © 1973, 1978, 1984 by International Bible Society. Used by permission of Zondervan. All rights reserved.

Produced in association with Educational Publishing Concepts, Inc.

The following trademarks used in the book are: Jiffy Pop® owned by INTERNATIONAL HOME FOODS, INC, Krispy Kreme® owned by HDN Development Corporation, and Cap'n Crunch® owned by Quaker Oats Company. None of the above-named companies have affiliation with Standard Publishing.

ISBN 0-7847-1738-9

12  11  10  09  08  07  06            9  8  7  6  5  4  3  2  1

Library of Congress Cataloging-in-Publication Data

Smouse, Phil A.
  You pray for me, I'll pray for you : tummy tickling stories and prayers we can read together / written and illustrated by Phil A. Smouse.
      p. cm. -- (Read together)
  ISBN 0-7847-1738-9 (casebound)
  1. Prayers--Juvenile literature. I. Title. II. Series.
  BV265.S66 2006
  242'.62--dc22
                            2005004002

This is the confidence we have in approaching God: that if we ask anything according to his will, he hears us. And if we know that he hears us—whatever we ask—we know that we have what we asked of him.

1 John 5:14, 15

**Well look at this!**

Here's something new.

**A book of stories built for two.**

I'll read orange.

**I'll read blue.**

We'll read the green
together too!

# For Mom and Dad

Little guys and gals love to talk to Jesus.

They talk to him about big important things. They talk to him about itsy-bitsy, teeny-weeny, silly little things that don't seem to matter much at all.

I guess that's why Jesus said the kingdom of Heaven belongs to them!

So go ahead and round up the little ones, snuggle up someplace warm and cozy, flip the page, and get ready for some tummy tickling fun.

Those cuddles and hugs and laughs and tickles and tiny little heartfelt words to the Father are always the very best part of the day.

# You Pray for Me, I'll Pray for You!

Good day.

Bonjour.

Shalom!

Hello.

It's time to
rise and shine.

I know!

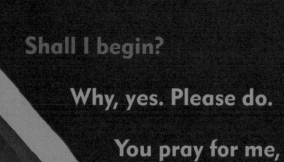

Shall I begin?

Why, yes. Please do.

You pray for me,
I'll pray for you!

11

Lord, use our lips
to bless and teach.

Lord, guard
our hearts.

Our hands.

Our feet.

Renew our minds.

Make all things new.

Please make us more
and more like YOU.

Lord, bless his night.

Lord, bless his day.

Lord, bless him each and every way.

Lord, give us strength to work and play.

Please let us touch your heart this day.

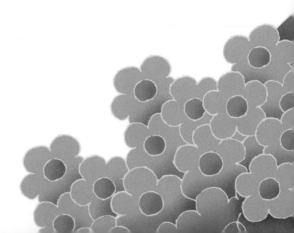

# You Are My Friend

You are my friend.

I like you best.

My heart is glad.

My life is blessed.

You make me smile.

You make me sing.

16

I love you more
than anything.

You say **DON'T STOP!**

You tell me **GO!**

You say **YOU CAN!**

You say **I KNOW.**

You make me strong.

You help me grow.

I love you more
than you can know.

I don't have much.

But I have you.

You are my friend.

You're my friend too.

# Alive!

**We need to hop.**

We need to bounce.

**We need to jump.**

We need to pounce.

**We need to leap.**

We need to spring.

**We need to dance.**

We need to sing!

Our hearts are his.

He took our sin.

He is ALIVE.

We're born again!

# We Need a Snack

Do you smell that?

That smell smells nice.

It smells like PIE.

With apple spice!

Or maybe butter biscuits.

Oooooooo.

With cinnamon
and sugar too!

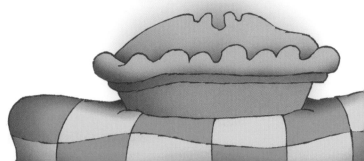

I think it's popcorn.

**Maybe steak.**

Peanut butter cookies.

**CAKE!**

Whipped cream.

**Waffles.**

Burgers.

**Fries!**

Thanksgiving dinner.

PUMPKIN PIE!

A freezer full of
soft ice cream.

A red hot box
from Krispy Kreme!®

A ten pound bag
of chocolate fudge.

We'll eat it all.

We'll never budge!

I think I even smell **TOFU!**

**TOFU?**
What's gotten into you?

We need a fork.

**We need a bowl.**

We need a little
self control.

**Oh, no, we don't.**

We need a SNACK!

You're right. We do!

I'll be right back.

# We Lost It

I lost my hat.

I lost my shoe.

I lost my glove.

I lost mine too.

I don't know what I'm going to do!

You pray for me, I'll pray for you!

31

I lost my belt.

Your pants may slip!

They won't if I don't
lose my grip.

32

My buttons popped.

Well, look at that.
Your belly's big
and round and fat.

I lost my glasses.

Check your head.

I think they fell
behind the bed.

34

Your head?

My glasses!

Cut that out!

That's one thing
I can't do without!

35

**What time is it?**

Who, me?

**Yes, you!**

I'll tell you in
a day or two.

**Why not right now?**

Right now won't do.
I think I lost
my marbles too!

You lost your marbles long ago.

Well, that explains a lot.

I know!

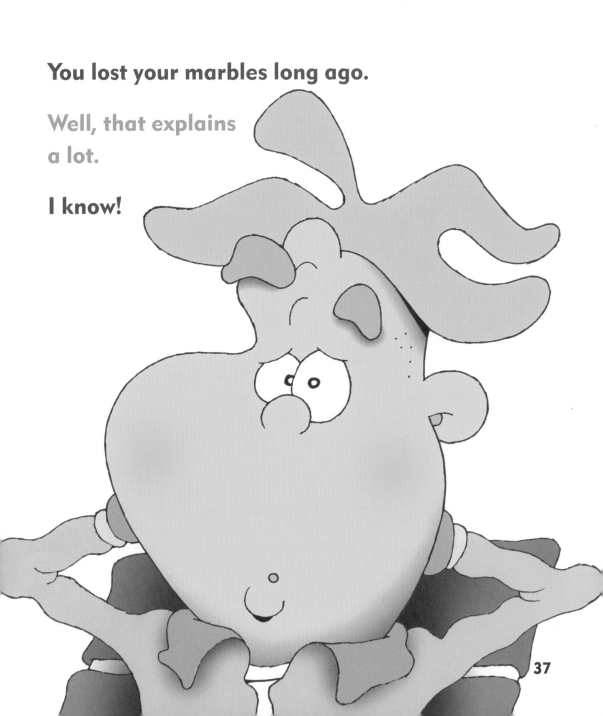

We're quite a mess.

**We're both a sight.**

It's no big deal.

**It's quite all right.**

Jesus loves us anyway.

**Let's tell him "Thanks!"**

Amen!

**Okay!**

At last we know just what to do:

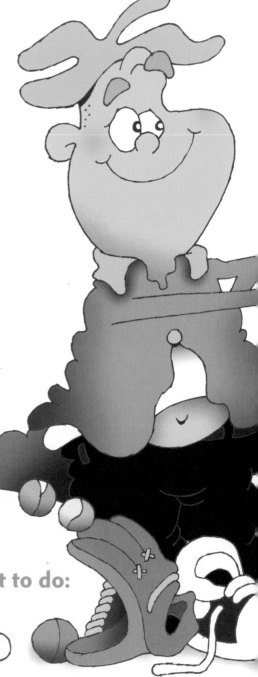

You pray for me,
I'll pray for you!

**I found my stuff.**

I found mine too!

**You did?**

I did!

**Good job.**

You too!

39

# Hurry Up!

**Hurry UP!**

Who, me?

**Yes, YOU!**
**You move too slow.**

I never knew.

**It's getting late.**
**We're stuck like glue.**
**You need to GO, GO, GO!**

I do?

41

**Come on. Get up!
Shove off. Heave HO!**

I will—
in half an hour or so.

**In HALF an HOUR?
We'll both be TOAST!**

But toast is what
I like the most.

With eggs and ham?

With jam and TEA!

Oh, no. It's rubbing off on ME!

I move too slow?

**YOU take TOO LONG.**

That's bad, bad, BAD?

**It's wrong, wrong, WRONG!**

You may be right.

**I always is.**

There's just one thing.

**Oh, no.**

There is?

45

What did you
need to do, do, do?

**I can't remember.**

No?

Can you?

You never said.

**Oh, no! It's true.**

You move too fast?

You're right.
I DO!

47

# We Can't Agree

I'm short.

I'm tall.

I'm fat.

I'm thin.

My ears stick out.

YOUR ears stick IN!

I like to run.

I like to walk.

I like to sleep.

I love to talk.

I like to slide.

I'd rather swing.

I want to dance.

I need to sing!

I make a fuss.

I'm calm and cool.

I like the beach.

I love the pool!

51

We're something else.

We're quite a pair.

We can't agree.

But we don't care!

You are my friend.

You're my friend too.

You pray for me,
I'll pray for you!

53

# Who Will Know?

I think we should.

We might get caught.

Let's do it now.

We better not.

They'll never know.

It isn't right.

We'll grab it and
duck out of sight!

So just this once?

**One little sin.**

And then we'll never
sin again?

**We'll mend our ways.**

We'll join the choir?

**We'll sing.**

Believe?

**Obey.**

Inspire!

Besides, it CAN'T be wrong.

IT'S FUN!

You're smart.

I know.

Good job!

Well done.

We did it now.

Oh, did we do!

There's no way out.

We're stuck like glue.

I feel like dirt.

Like muck.

Like goo.

I want to change.

I want that too.

There IS a way.

I know.

You do?

You pray for me,
I'll pray for you!

59

# Time for Bed

It's time for bed.

Turn out the light.

Okay, I will.

Good night.

Good night.

Your feet are cold.

Oh, no, they're not!

They're not?

They're not.
My feet are HOT!

My feet are still
inside my shoes!

Then whose are these?

Those feet are Lou's.

Well, how did Lou get in here too?

You let him in.

Did not.

Did too!

63

Did you hear that?

Hear what?

That sound!

That squeaking,

Creaking,

Slinking,

Sneaking,

Heartbeat stopping,

Goose bump popping . . .

**Stop! I'm scared!**

Now I'm scared too!

**There's only one thing left to do.**

Let's do it now!

**You start.**

No, you!

# One of Them

**Do you love Jesus?**

Yes, I do.

**You're one of THEM!**

I'm one of who?

**A JESUS FREAK.**

I'm one of THOSE?

**You just may be.**

Well, Heaven knows!

Your eyes are WILD.

My mind's at rest.

You've popped your cork.

My life is blessed.

You've flipped your lid.

I shout AMEN!

You're lost in space.

I'm born again!

You go to church.

I love God's Word.

You're daffy as
a dodo bird.

I'm twice as sweet
as Cap'n Crunch®?

That's what I said.

Well, thanks a bunch!

71

I guess you're right.
I'm one of **THOSE**.

**I KNEW IT!**

That's the way
it goes.

**You're born again!**

Both tried and true.

# A JESUS FREAK!

Well, how about YOU?

# Mad, mad, MAD!

I'm mad!

You're mad?

I'm mad,
mad,
MAD!

That's nothing new.

This time it's BAD.

Well, I'm mad too.

You are?

It's true.

You're mad
at what?

I'M MAD
AT YOU!

You're mad
at ME?
That isn't fair!

I know.

You do?

But I don't
care.

It WASN'T me!

It WAS.

You're sure?

You bet I am.

Then this means
WAR!

You bite your nails.

You play with blocks.

You smell like cheese.

You chew your socks.

Your face is RED.

Your face is BLUE.

Your eyes bug out.

Yours bug out too!

We're going to BLOW.

We're going to POP.

We're going to pop
if we don't STOP!

LORD, HELP, BEFORE WE
BLOW OUR TOPS JUST LIKE
A BAG OF JIFFY POP!®

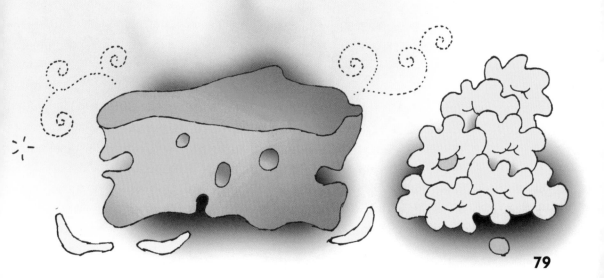

What made you mad?

You took my hat.

That wasn't me.

No?

That was Pat.

Then I'm not mad.

I'm glad.

Me too.

But you still
smell like cheese.

81

# I'm Feeling Better Too

I stubbed my toe.

I scraped my knee.

I bumped my head.

Oh, woe is me!

I need to sneeze.

I have to cough.

I think my nose
just shot right off.

My eyebrows itch.

**My cheeks don't work.**

My belly button's
gone berserk.

**My lips are chapped.**

My teeth are too.

**My hair is turning
black and blue!**

I can't get up.

**I can't sit down.**

The room is spinning
round and round!

**I have a FROG
down in my throat!**

That's not a frog.
You have a **GOAT!**

BOO
BOOZ

**A GOAT? I don't.**

Oh, yes, you do!
Just have a look.

**I can't.**

Says who?

**My mom.**

Your MOM?

**She told me don't.**

Well, if your mom
says don't, we won't.

How IS your mom?

**Her nose is stuffed.**

It is? Mine too.
It's pink and puffed.

**Both sides?**

Oh, no. It's just the right.

**The left?**

The left is
plugged up tight.

**You said the left
was working fine!**

Do you mean yours
or hers or mine?

**We're quite a mess.**

That's plain to see.

We need to pray.

**You're telling me!**

Then let's get to it.

**While we're young . . .**

Oh, dear!

What's wrong?

I bit my tongue.

Why, yes, you did.
Just look at that.
Your tongue is getting
big and fat!

Thtop teathing me!
You thaid you'd pway!

You're right. I did.

Stho pway, otay?

Okay. Here's what we're going to do.

You pray for me, I'll pray for you!

I'm feeling better.
How about you?

**Guess what?**
**I'm feeling better too!**

# I Ripped My Pants

I ripped my pants!

You ripped them good.

I need to hide.

I think you should.

My mom will **FLIP.**

That may be true.

**I KNOW** she will.
These pants are **NEW.**

So get another
pair of pants.

Another pair?

Of course.

Fat chance.

You wore your NEW
pants out to play?

I ripped my
old pants yesterday.

93

Your mom will **FLIP!**

**My mom will GROWL!**

Your mom will
bark and scream.

**And HOWL!**

Your goose is cooked.

**I'm toast.**

OH, WOW. You're really
going to get it now.

TIMBUKTU

I can't go home.

What will you do?

I'll have to move to Timbuktu.

You'll run away?

I'll hop a plane.

You hate to fly.

I'll take the train.

The train may jump
right off the track.

I'll play it safe
and take a yak.

A yak will give
your legs a rash.

They'll burn and sting?

They'll itch and scratch.

That isn't good.

You'll smell bad too.

# Then what am I supposed to do?

I think that you
should tell your mom.

**Go spill the beans?**

Just drop the bomb.

**That never works.
I know. I've tried.**

But a hole like that is hard to hide.

So I'll tell the truth.

She won't be mad.

She'll laugh.

You'll pray.

We'll both be glad.

Let's go, okay?

I'll follow you.

OH, NO!

WHAT NOW?

I broke my shoe!

# Loot or Scoot

**I think it's time.**

What time is that?

**It's time for you-know-what!**

Oh, that.

**You'd like to then?**

Why, yes. Let's do!

**Let's have a snack.**

A snack for two.

What do you want?

Let's have ice cream.

Ice cream! That sounds just like a dream.

Oh, good. It looks like we're in luck.

You're right! Here comes the ice cream truck.

Oh, no.

**What's wrong?**

Well, don't you know?
The ice cream man
will want some dough.

**Some dough?**

Some dough.
Some loot! Some cash!

**Let's check our pockets,
now, and fast!**

I don't have loot or cash or dough.

What do you have?

I have to go!

You can't go now.
We'll miss the truck.
Without your loot
we're out of luck!

We're out of luck?

Without your loot.

Without my loot?

We'll have to scoot!

Oh, look.

**At what?**

Oh, my!

**Oh, no!**

I'm not so sure
you want to know.

**I do! I do!
What did you spot?**

Okay. Let's see.
Here's what we've got:

A top. A rock. A paper clip.

**A greasy green potato chip.**

A dried up bug.

**A ball of lint.**

Two toe nails and a hairy mint!

**I don't think that
will buy ice cream.**

You may be right.

**I'm going to scream.**

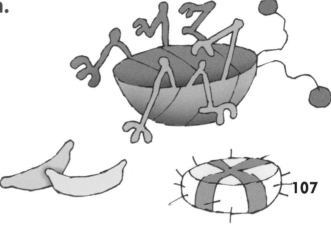

Oh, don't do that.

**There goes the truck!**

Hey, look! I just found
half a buck.

My tummy hurts.
My head does too.

You know what we forgot to do?

I'd love to know.

I think you do.

We should have done it first?

How true!

Go right ahead.

Please, after you . . .

You pray for me,
I'll pray for you!

**Was that our mom?**

Why, yes, it was.
She says she has ICE CREAM!

# I Quit

**That's it. I QUIT!**

You CAN'T quit now.

**I've had enough.**

You have? But HOW?
You can't just walk away.

**Can too.**

We'll never be the same!

**Says who?**

I need your hands.

**My hands are beat.**

I need your feet.

**They can't compete.**

I need your arms.

**My arms have drooped.**

I need your brains.

**My brains are pooped.**

I need your hugs.

**My HUGS? You DO?**

I LOVE you.

**YOU love ME?**

I DO.

THANKS FOR VISITING SCENIC
MT. SLUSHMORE

MAXIMUM SPEED: MACH 5.
THANKS FOR NOT GETTING
TOO UPSET ABOUT THAT SIGN
ON THE PREVIOUS PAGE.

HAVE A NICE DAY

I'm sorry that I yelled all day.

I promise not to go away.

I'd never make it without you.

I love you.

And I love you too.

# Let's Never Fight

Hey, that's my shirt!

Hey, that's my hat!

You've got my glove!

You've got my bat!

You touched my bike!

You're on my dirt!

You pushed me down!

It didn't hurt!

**Oh, yes, it did. You pushed me first.**

My push was first,
but yours was worse.

You got some mud up in my nose!

That isn't mud.

You're really gross!

121

You make me MAD!

**Well, I'm mad too!**

I wish you'd
go away!

You do?

You're really nice.

I like you too.

Let's never fight.

Oh, I'm with you.

From now on
when we start to stew,

You pray for me.
I'll pray for you!

# I Do

We need to pray.

Who, me?

Yes, you.

Do you think
Jesus hears?

I do!

He's here right now.

Inside this room?

Inside your heart.

Inside yours too?

And we can
tell him anything.

He won't get mad?

His heart will sing!

So when I'm happy,

When I'm sad,

When I get hurt,

Or when I'm MAD,

When I'm afraid,

Or when I'm blue,

You pray for me,
I'll pray for you!

I love Jesus.

**I do too.**

And he loves me.

**I love you too!**

129

# A Perfect Day

Today was nice.

Today was fun.

I'd like to have
another one.

Another perfect day.

Or two!

130

You'll be with me?

I'll be with you.

Let's wake up early.

**That sounds great.**

I'll meet you
right back here.

**At eight!**

You're my best friend.

**You're my best too.**

I'm glad I have
a friend like you.

**Good nighty night.**

Good night to you.

**Sweet dreams.**

Sleep tight.

**I will.**

Me too.

**I love you, friend.**

I love you too.

**Let's pray, okay?**

Okay. Let's do!

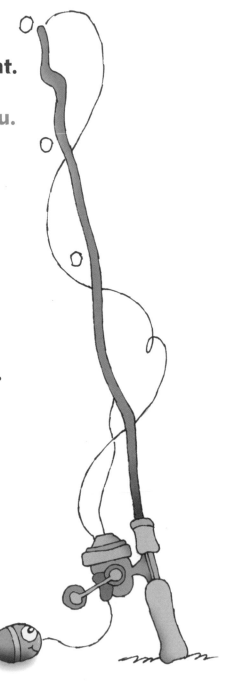

Lord, thank you for this perfect day.
This day was good in every way.
Our minds can rest. Our hearts can sing.
We love you more than anything.

# Good Night!

**Good night!**

Bonsoir.

**Shalom.**

Adieu.

**It's to time say good night.**

Oh, foo!

Shall I begin?

Why, yes. Please do.

You pray for me,
I'll pray for you!

Lord, bless his head.

Lord, bless his feet.

Lord, guard his heart.

Lord, grant him sleep.

Lord, bless his dreams.

Lord, let him snore.

But first please let me
close the door!

Lord, bless his pillow.

Bless his clothes.

Lord, bless that stuff
between his toes.

Without you, Jesus,
we're a mess.

But thanks to you,

Our lives are blessed!

Good night.

Bonsoir.

Shalom.

Adieu.

I wish I could speak
French.

Me too!

You pray for me,
I'll pray for you!

# What is Prayer?

When you talk to God with your own words,
when you tell him everything that's on your heart,
you are praying—and God is listening!

It doesn't matter where you are.
It doesn't matter what you are doing.
Jesus loves you.
You can tell him anything.
Why don't you talk to him right now?

Do you like to write?
Do you love to draw?
Is your head full of silly stories too?

Mr. Smouse would love to hear from you today!

So get out your crayons and markers
and send a letter, a picture, a story,
or anything else for that matter, to:

Phil A. Smouse,
Standard Publishing
8121 Hamilton Avenue
Cincinnati, OH 45231

And the good folks at Standard
will be sure to pass it along.

You can also visit my web site: philsmouse.com